# Good Housekeeping
# NEW
# COOKING

# Good Housekeeping
# NEW
# COOKING

## THE **ULTIMATE** GUIDE TO **CONTEMPORARY** COOKING WITH OVER **500** RECIPES

TED SMART

A Ted Smart Publication 2000

First published 1999

1 3 5 7 9 10 8 6 4 2

First published in the United Kingdom in 1999 by Ebury Press
Random House · 20 Vauxhall Bridge Road · London SW1V 2SA

Random House Australia (Pty) Limited
20 Alfred Street · Milsons Point · Sydney · New South Wales 2061 · Australia

Random House New Zealand Limited
18 Poland Road · Glenfield · Auckland 10 · New Zealand

Random House South Africa (Pty) Limited
Endulini · 5A Jubilee Road · Parktown 2193 · South Africa

The Random House Group Limited Reg. No. 954009

www.randomhouse.co.uk

A CIP catalogue record for this book is available from the British Library.

Papers used by Ebury Press are natural, recyclable products made from wood grown in sustainable forests.

Managing Editor: Janet Illsley
Design: Lovelock & Co.

Photographs: Jean Cazals, Laurie Evans, David Gill, Graham Kirk, Sandra Lousada, James Murphy, Philip Webb, Harry Cory-Wright, Elizabeth Zeschin

Recipes: The Good Housekeeping Institute, Joanna Farrow, Louise Pickford, Maxine Clark, Lyn Rutherford, Janet Smith, Linda Fraser

Additional editorial assistance: Hilary Bird, Kim Griffiths

Colour reproduction by CST-COLORLITO, Milan

Printed and bound in Slovenia by Mladinska knjiga Tiskarna, d.d.
by arangement with Korotan – Ljubljana d.o.o.

# contents

## cookery notes

- Both metric and imperial measures are given for the recipes. Follow either set of measures, not a mixture of both, as they are not interchangeable.
- All spoon measures are level unless otherwise stated. Use measuring spoons, available in metric and imperial, for accurate quantities.
- Ovens must be preheated to the specified temperature. Grills should also be preheated. Cooking times in the recipes are based on this assumption.
- Large eggs should be used except where otherwise specified. Free-range eggs are recommended.
- Use freshly ground black pepper and sea salt unless otherwise specified.
- Use fresh rather than dried herbs unless dried herbs are stipulated.
- If a recipe uses grated lemon rind, or pared zest, buy unwaxed lemons.

The recipes include the following information:
- Preparation and cooking times, plus additional time for proving etc.
- Suitability for freezing. Where the dish should be frozen at the end of a certain stage of the method (rather than at the end), this stage is indicated.
- Calorie counts are given per serving or appropriate portion of the dish. Where the calorie count ranges from a higher to a lower figure, this reflects that the number the recipe serves is variable. The lower count will apply if you are serving the larger number, as the portion size will be smaller.

# the basics of new cooking

Lifestyles today are invariably busy – with children to take care of, a job to be juggled, and a host of other demands – time for shopping and cooking is necessarily limited. Contemporary cooking, therefore, needs to reflect this reality as well as respond to the continuing need for a diet that is healthy and varied, as well as tasty. To help achieve these objectives, follow the simple guidelines that follow.

## balance your diet

We are often told to eat healthily, but are rarely told how to do so. There is no great secret: to maintain good health we need to provide our bodies with nutrition in the form of regular amounts of protein, vitamins, minerals, fibre and carbohydrate, and small amounts of fat.

**protein** helps keep skin, teeth, internal organs and other tissues healthy, and food provides most of the body's needs. The best sources are meat, poultry, fish, eggs, dairy foods and soya.

**vitamins** are necessary for many body processes and a shortage can lead to poor health. Vitamins A, B, C, D, E and K are obtained from food (although the best source of vitamin D is sunlight). Leafy vegetables and grains, among other foods, contain several different vitamins.

**minerals** are required in small quantities, particularly iron, calcium and zinc. Meat and leafy green vegetables are rich in iron, calcium is found in dairy foods and oily fish, while lean meat, seafood and grains contain zinc.

**fibre** is vital to a healthy digestive system. Unrefined cereals, bran, fresh vegetables and fruit all contain fibre – in fact, if you start the day with wholegrain cereal and eat plenty of fresh fruit and vegetables during the course of it, you will have enough fibre in your diet.

**carbohydrates** provide energy. Sugar carbohydrates are present in fruit, milk and sugar, while potatoes, cereals, pasta, grains and pulses all contain starch carbohydrates. Starch carbohydrates should always provide a higher proportion of your energy requirements than sugar ones since they provide essential nutrients.

**fat** provides heat and energy. There are three types: saturated, monosaturated and polyunsaturated. The more saturated fat you eat, the more unhealthy, potentially, you could become. Dairy products (especially butter and cream) are high in saturated fat, as are red meats; olive oil is a monosaturated fat while other oils, such as groundnut and corn, and oily fish, are rich in polyunsaturated fat.

## eat a balanced diet

If you eat a balanced diet, your body will receive all the nutrients it needs to maintain good health and you shouldn't need vitamin and mineral supplements (unless you suffer excessive loss of certain nutrients, perhaps due to pregnancy, illness or infirmity). Avoid adding salt to cooked food; if you miss the taste, try substituting fresh herbs. If you eat some foods from each of the following categories every day, your diet will be a healthy one.

**cereals and grains** such as bread, pasta, rice and breakfast cereals provide energy, fibre, B vitamins, calcium and iron.

**fruit and vegetables** are a good source of vitamins, particularly A and C, and minerals, particularly iron and calcium.

### healthy shortcuts

Convenience foods can form part of a healthy eating lifestyle – if you choose and use them wisely.

- Buy grilled or baked dishes rather than fried ones.

- Serve ready-made main courses with plenty of freshly cooked vegetables or salad.

- For fast meals, buy ready-chopped fresh vegetables and use as part of a meal, such as a stir-fry.

- Buy ready-prepared mixed salad and use with fresh dressing as an accompaniment to a main course or, with canned tuna and hard-boiled eggs, to make a summer meal.

- Enlarge your repertoire of 'instant' recipes – you will be much less tempted to buy ready-made meals if you have a variety of easily prepared fresh recipe ideas to hand.

**meat, poultry and fish** are valuable sources of protein, energy and iron. Eat mostly white meats such as chicken, turkey and game, but balance with a little red meat once or twice a week. If possible eat fish, especially oily fish, at least twice a week.

**dairy products** are good for protein, energy, calcium, minerals, vitamins D and B12, but use richer dairy foods, such as butter, eggs and cream, in moderation. Skimmed milk contains all the nutrients of whole milk without the fat.

**pulses, nuts and seeds** provide protein, energy, fibre, calcium, iron and zinc.

**water** helps flush out impurities in your system. Five glasses a day (including fruit juices, but not tea and coffee) will keep you healthy.

**vegetarians** need a varied diet, just as meat-eaters do. Variety, in fact, is particularly important if you are a vegetarian because some vegetable proteins lack essential amino acids (the small units that make up proteins). By eating certain foods together, however, particularly vegetables with grains, this problem can be overcome. Combinations, such as pulses with rice, vegetables and nuts with couscous, and cereal with milk, are as tasty as they are healthy. A vegan diet is more restricted than a vegetarian one since it does not contain dairy produce, and usually lacks vitamin B12. To compensate, vegans should eat fortified breakfast cereal, yeast extract and soya products, including soy sauce and tofu, as part of their diet.

**ready-prepared foods** are a great temptation, but when it comes to a healthy diet, the old adage 'fresh is best' says it all. There are very few of us who don't pop a ready meal into the microwave from time to time. So long as this is sometimes rather than often, there's no harm done, but prepared meals tend to contain high amounts of salt and should not form the basis of anyone's diet. Some takeaway foods such as fish and chips can be high in saturated fats and are best eaten occasionally rather than often. Alternate with Indian (especially tandoori dishes), and Chinese food, which usually contain vegetables.

# get the most from shopping

Organise your shopping as well as you can: go to the supermarket outside usual hours to avoid endless checkout queuing, plan your week's meals as far as possible, and make a shopping list before you go. If you want to be really organised, pack your purchases into separate bags at the checkout according to where you will store them when you get home. Use local greengrocers, butchers, fishmongers and markets for fresh food top-ups.

Good cooking is all about good shopping: buying fresh food in good condition, knowing which cuts of meat to buy, recognising when fruit or vegetables are properly ripe. Always buy the best you can afford, preferably in its natural season when it will taste better and cost less. Often this means buying organic produce – meat, vegetables and fruit created without using synthetic feed, pesticides or artificial fertilizers – even though it is more expensive.

Nearly all supermarkets now stock organic vegetables and fruit and most also sell organic chickens, eggs and other dairy products. Many greengrocers and butchers also specialise in local organic produce. Organic produce is worth looking for: even everyday vegetables like potatoes or carrots can taste better, while there is simply no comparison between organic chickens and their bland conventional counterparts. Owing to the slight risk of salmonella, always buy eggs from a reliable source with a fast turnover. This is most important if you are using them uncooked, say in a homemade mayonnaise, or lightly cooked in a carbonara sauce.

# organise your food storage

Almost everything we buy needs to be stored, even food to be eaten that day. For vegetables and fruit, remove them from their plastic bags and store in a cool place, preferably away from direct sunlight. Keep day-to-day perishables, such as opened jams and mayonnaise in the refrigerator, along with dairy produce, fresh and cooked meat and fish (always keep fresh meat and fish on separate shelves to cooked items). Salad vegetables and perishable vegetables should be kept at the bottom of the refrigerator. Store emergency loaves of bread as well as the usual staples of vegetables, ice cream and chips in the freezer.

# stock your storecupboard

The contents of your storecupboard will depend on your personal preferences. As a rule of thumb when stocking it, however, try always to have the makings of an impromptu meal or two plus the basis of several more, as well as providing basic everyday staples. Most storecupboard items will last a long time, but keep an eye on 'use by' dates, and make sure you have a regular turnover of items. The following list could act as a general guideline.

## use your freezer

With a little forward planning, the freezer can virtually function as an extra storecupboard.

- Keep a selection of ingredients that can be cooked straight from frozen – pitta bread, peas, sweetcorn, sliced bread (for toast), and oven chips are all good examples.

- Store a selection of ready-made pastry doughs – these thaw quickly and can form the basis of many main courses and puddings. Puff and filo pastry are particularly useful as they are exceptionally good and otherwise time-consuming to make.

- Tubs of fresh stock can be cooked from frozen if you do not use them fresh; or boil down leftover stock and freeze in ice cube trays to use instead of stock cubes. Concentrated fruit juices can be frozen in the same way, then reconstituted into instant cold drinks or used in desserts.

- Make double quantities when you are cooking pasta sauces or stews, and freeze for another meal.

**pasta** is perfect for fast midweek suppers, so stock a selection of good quality dried varieties. Keep some ribbon pasta, such as tagliatelle, at least one long strand pasta, such as spaghetti, plus some short ones, such as penne or fusilli, and some precooked lasagne sheets. Children are usually keen on multi-coloured spiral shapes.

**rice, grains and pulses** form the basis of many dishes. Rice comes in many varieties: long-grain white and brown rice, plus risotto rice are the basics; for more information on good speciality rices to store, see page 162. Grains can also be used to provide good carbohydrate – see page 166 for a useful selection. If you like Indian food or hearty soups, keep a supply of lentils. Green or brown varieties are often used in curries, while red ones can be used in curries or to bulk out hearty soups. Puy lentils are also green but have a distinctive taste, quite different from conventional green lentils.

**oils and vinegars** should be stored at the back of the cupboard to protect them from heat and light, and olive oil is best bought in dark green bottles for the same reason. Use oils for cooking in preference to butter, as a lighter alternative. Keep good-quality vegetable oil if you deep-fry, light olive oil for other cooking and extra virgin olive oil for salad dressings. For a change of taste, walnut oil could be used for dressings, and also for cooking vegetables (it goes particularly well with green beans). If you cook Chinese food regularly, sesame oil is a must.

White and red wine vinegars are the staple vinegars and can be used for a variety of purposes. Balsamic and sherry vinegars are also a must for many people now; use in cooking (add either one to calf's liver, for instance) or in salad dressings. Stock malt vinegar if you make your own chutneys and pickles, and of course it is the essential adjunct to fish and chips.

**flours and sugars** once opened, are best stored in airtight containers that can be accessed easily with spoons or measures. The amount and variety of flour you will need depends on whether you bake regularly or not, but you will need some plain white or wholemeal flour (for thickening gravies and coating fish or meat). Cornflour can also be useful, particularly if you cook Chinese food regularly. Types of sugar will also depend on your family's preferences. Granulated white and brown sugar, caster sugar and icing sugar are the basics.

**baking ingredients** If you bake regularly, keep baking powder, bicarbonate of soda and cream of tartar. If you bake bread, stock some fast-acting yeast, and powdered gelatine is needed for making mousses and other 'set' desserts. Other essential ingredients include good quality chocolate (see page 344), golden syrup, thin honey and cocoa powder. A selection of special cake accessories, such as marzipan and food colouring, could also come in handy for making birthday and Christmas cakes.

**dried fruit and nuts** make nutritious snacks as well as adding interest to many savoury and sweet dishes, and baked items. Store in airtight containers once opened – nuts in particular stale quickly. Vacuum-packed chestnuts and prunes are useful; and if you bake, have to hand some walnut halves, slivered almonds, raisins, sultanas and candied cherries.

**cans, jars and packets** always merit space in the storecupboard. The choice will depend on taste, although some basics are indispensable. Cans of plum tomatoes, for instance, will form the basis of stews and pasta sauces, jars of passata can be used for the same purpose, as can small tins of tomato paste. Sun-dried tomato paste is another staple that can be used in this way: the flavour is intense and a spoonful or two will add richness to many dishes. Ready-made pesto, sold in jars, can form the basis of a pasta meal on its own, or add flavour to sauces and risottos; you can now buy olive and red pepper pestos as well as the classic basil variety.

Cans of vegetables, particularly different types of beans, are also always useful. Canned tuna is a versatile standby, while canned soups make good emergency meals, and canned consommé makes an excellent rich stock.

Encourage your children to eat cereals for breakfast by offering a selection of different types, avoiding sugar-coated ones for the sake of their teeth (or at least restricting these to weekends). Dried pulses, such as kidney and haricot beans, and chick peas, have their place even though they require long cooking times. Dried mushrooms are excellent for enhancing the flavour of stews and pasta sauces, particularly porcini mushrooms or ceps; use their soaking water as a strongly flavoured basis for vegetarian stocks. A few packets of stock cubes could be useful for emergencies, and if you like Indian food, keep some blocks of creamed coconut or cans of coconut milk.

## natural partners

All herbs enhance the flavour of food, but some combinations go particularly well together (see below). To bring out the full flavour, use fresh herbs and stir into a cooked dish just before serving unless the recipe specifically says otherwise. For a list of good salad herbs, see page 73.

BASIL is ideal with tomatoes, tomato sauces and grills

BAY, PARSLEY AND THYME to make bouquet garni, soups and stocks, barbecues, particularly kebabs

CORIANDER with curried, middle eastern and Mexican dishes, aubergines, seafood, especially shrimp

DILL enhances fish, especially salmon, delicate white sauces, and vegetables such as carrots

MINT perks up vegetables, especially potatoes and peas, lamb, yogurt, middle eastern and Indian dishes

PARSLEY partners most savoury foods, but especially white fish and seafood such as shrimp, vegetables (especially potatoes), sauces and soups

ROSEMARY marries well with lamb, chicken, meat marinades, roast potatoes and flavoured vinegar

SAGE goes with pork, stuffings, liver and dried beans

TARRAGON has a distinctive flavour, best reserved for chicken, omelettes and flavoured vinegar

**condiments and flavourings** are essential. Stock a few different mustards for salad dressings, cooking and as a relish – keep powdered English for cooking, plus wholegrain or Dijon for salad dressings, steaks and ham. No home should be without tomato ketchup and Worcestershire sauce, marvellous with cooked food and also to use in cooking: in homemade burgers, for instance, or cottage pie. Soy sauce is also a necessity, both dark and light – use for dressings and marinades as well as in stir-fries and fish grills.

Spices are another must, but always buy in small quantities so that your supply remains fresh. In the essential category are black peppercorns and salt – sea salt for preference, since it is rich in magnesium. A selection of Indian spices should also find a spot on your shelf: your preferred strength of curry powder, plus jars of cumin, coriander, turmeric, cayenne and chilli powder. For a stronger taste buy cumin and coriander in seed form and grind to use. Crushed chilli flakes and jars of different ready-made curry pastes are also useful. For sweet flavours, stock cinnamon sticks (and powder), whole nutmegs, vanilla pods, almond and vanilla extracts.

Herbs are best grown and used fresh or bought fresh from your greengrocer or supermarket, but a few dried ones are worth stocking for emergencies: dried oregano, dried mixed herbs and herbes de provence, for instance, can cheer up omelettes, or flavour meat sauces. Remember that dried herbs are stronger than fresh, so use sparingly.

## cook sensibly

Contemporary cooking relies primarily on a few well chosen pieces of equipment. At the top of the list is a good selection of different-sized saucepans, preferably non-stick cast iron or stainless steel – non-stick pans help cut down on the amounts of oil you use for cooking. A steamer is also a necessity; steaming helps to preserve nutrients in vegetables better than boiling and is an excellent method of cooking delicate fish.

A sturdy wok also makes life easier – and don't just keep it for stir-fries; its efficient shape means that it can be easily adapted to any type of one-pot cooking. Pasta sauces can be cooked in it, for instance, the pasta added at the last minute and tossed to coat properly. If you invest in a bamboo steamer, a wok can also be adapted into a temporary steamer.

A microwave oven can also transform what is possible in the kitchen. Use as an adjunct to the freezer to thaw ready-prepared food or to reheat quickly, or as a way to cut down long cooking times. Children like using microwaves, and teaching them to use it is often a good way of getting them interested in cooking generally.

In summer, barbecues are healthy and fun. At other times of the year, use the grill rather than your frying pan to cook chops, sausages and fish. For oven use, you will need a strong roasting pan, preferably non-stick, and a casserole dish or two, one of which should be flameproof.

Kitchen accessories can also help: a food processor makes many otherwise complicated dishes accessible: mayonnaise, for instance, becomes simple to make, and the time-consuming tasks of rubbing-in pastry, chopping vegetables and mixing dough, for example, are eliminated. Good knives are also a must: at least two for preparing vegetables and meat, plus a serrated-edged knife for cutting bread and a carving knife. You should also find a place for kitchen foil: use it to line the grill pan when you cook, to parcel food to steam in the oven, and to store items in the freezer. Many other kitchen items can help too, depending on your tastes: a garlic press, a grinder to make fresh coffee powder, an ice-cream maker, even a pasta maker.

All of the above help make it easier to serve good food. And good, tasty, healthy food is the foundation, not only of new cooking, but of good family health and well-being, too.